The Ninjas

JANE YEH was born in America an[...] holds master's degrees from the Io[...] Metropolitan University. Her prev[...] Carcanet in 2005 and shortlisted for the Whitbread Poetry [...] Forward Prize for Best First Collection, and the Jerwood Aldeburgh First Collection Prize. Her chapbook *Teen Spies* was published in 2003 by Metre Editions. She is the recipient of a New York Foundation for the Arts Fellowship and an Academy of American Poets Prize. Currently teaching at Kingston University, she also contributes articles on books, theatre, fashion and sport to *The Times Literary Supplement*, *Poetry Review*, *Time Out* and *The Village Voice*. She lives in London.

JANE YEH

The Ninjas

CARCANET

Acknowledgements

Sincere thanks to the editors of the anthologies, publications, and websites where some of these poems first appeared: *The Best British Poetry 2012*, *Boston Review*, *Edinburgh Review*, likestarlings.com, *Lung Jazz: Young British Poets for Oxfam*, *The Nation*, *New Welsh Review*, *PN Review*, *Poetry Ireland Review*, *Poetry Review*, *Poetry Wales*, *The Warwick Review*, and *Women's Studies Quarterly*. Thanks also to the judges of the following competitions: 'Musk-Ox' was awarded the 2012 Jane Martin Poetry Prize. The first section of 'Sargent's *The Daughters of Edward D. Boit*', subtitled 'Four Sisters', won third prize in the 2011 Edwin Morgan International Poetry Competition. 'The Body in the Library' received a commendation in the 2009 National Poetry Competition.

The author gratefully acknowledges the support of the Corporation of Yaddo and its grant of an artist's residency in 2010.

First published in Great Britain in 2012 by
Carcanet Press Limited
Alliance House
Cross Street
Manchester M2 7AQ

www.carcanet.co.uk

A CIP catalogue record for this book is available from the British Library

ISBN 978 1 84777 147 6

The publisher acknowledges financial assistance from Arts Council England

Typeset by XL Publishing Services, Tiverton
Printed and bound in England by SRP Ltd, Exeter

Contents

III

I

After the Attack of the Crystalline Entity

There were escape pods everywhere.
There was rasping.

Craters, shards, rivers, and voids.

Everywhere people were running into tunnels.
Voles *weren't* in the tunnels.
Where did all the voles go?

There was a shoe on the pavement, a metal hand,
Unreplicated litter, some kind of space-mat.

Only half of me still exists.

The next day, I swept up in the lab,
Made myself a new charging station out of scraps.
As a masterless man, I have more responsibilities.

This is an experiment I just devised:
Fireball and rat in a glass tube,
First one to reach home wins.
Behind home plate is a catcher made of stakes.

I can see outside if I bother to look.
Outside looks like the inside of everyone's houses
Dumped inside out. Outside, the air

Leaks bad particles into people's blood.
Luckily my self-filtering larynx keeps me safe.

Inside the lab, I can talk to myself
Without anyone noticing. I can make a rabbit
Turn blue, then back again. I took the limbs

Of a cat and moved them around
The room. This is an experiment on
Myself: how many days does it take

To give up waiting for anyone to come home?

Sargent's *The Daughters of Edward D. Boit*

1 Four Sisters

Each girl has got her best dress on.
At dawn, they were washed and brushed and tied
Into pinnies. Then the long wait

Until afternoon, when their florid mamá
Peers in for a moment; is off to the coiffeur's.
The one on the floor wants to know what her doll

Thinks about being painted. The one in the door just wants
To cut her hair short. The one on the side is trying
Her hardest not to fall over. The last one

Dreams herself into colour a limb at a time.
Her eyes look dubious. If the world
Makes us pay for our pleasure, how much will she owe?

Her aberrant shadow trails her like a servant.
Her beruffled wrists know no compulsion.
Her indolent sash is a cascading sigh.

She won't marry for love, or money.
She'll found a museum for unmanufacturable inventions.
She can't let them find out where, or why.

2 One Sister

I still play with dolls, but I know they're just pretend. My best friend
Is the housekeeper's cat. We are both exceptionally

Refined: he only eats mackerel, from a porcelain bowl.
I only wear silk taffeta ribbons on my head. He sounds like

A small growling dog when he purrs. I sound like a lady
Dog yapping, Mrs Locke says. If I were a lady cat

I could use my claws to unhook the pink strings
Of my sisters' stays. I could slowly wave my tail in the air

To mean *Give me some cream pie* or *What is the height
Of Faneuil Hall as measured in cats?* My triangular skull

Would fit exactly into Mrs Locke's hand. She thinks
Our family's a silly thing, like putting a pug dog into

A party dress. She doesn't know I sometimes put her cat
In the bathroom sink – he likes it there.

What *I* think: when my sisters are grown up
I'll still be at home, not old enough yet.

If I close my eyes for a second, the world seems to end.
If I had a brother, we could run up and down

The hall all day, then build a castle for the cat.
When all of us are old, nobody we know now will be left.

3   Recipe for a Painting

A pair of giant blue and white vases.
Darkness.
Four corners of a square.
Red ribbon looped in an intricate bow.
(The carpet makes a pale base for his operations.)
Preposterous blocking.
Between shadows, shadows.
Uncertain atmosphere of mirth, ennui, suspended doubt, and likeness.
Eight eyeballs looking around the room.
Horsehair and metal on a wooden stick.
Curled hair going limp.
The sound of day falling.

4 Playing Dead

The girls crowd round his easel like frilly pigeons,
Chattering. The allure of children
Escapes him – they seem

To be everywhere. He waits
For them to stretch, scratch, yawn, pull on
Each other's hems, then puts them back in their places

Again. They like this game
Of posing, just like they like to play
The game Playing Dead – one of them

Lies flat on the settee,
Holding her breath; two are the mourners
All dressed in black; the last is the ghost come back

From the grave, like an extra twin left over
In a womb. They wait for someone
To stop them, for the clocks

In the house to turn, the laced
Fingers of the afternoon to undo
Their sentence. An incomplete sentence

Is missing its feet. An unfinished painting
Has only heads and groundstrokes where the world
Should be. The painting ends with the girls released –

They vanish, leaving their faces behind like masks
On the empty canvas. He starts to bind the night
Into the size of a room.

He can't sleep because of the pendulum in his head.
His favourite medium is twilight.
He doesn't know if he'll find a mate in time to save him.

On Being an Android

My positronic hair never grows an inch.
(It looks like hair, but it's made of wires.)
My brain doesn't look like a brain, but it doesn't matter.
My friends think of me as reliable because I never get sick.
My hands can be used to unscrew bolts and pull things from the oven.

How I was made: equal parts mystery and on-off switches.
Age 5: driving lessons, triathlon, med school, embroidery.
Everyone says looks don't matter, as long as you've got personality.
My first crush was a Roomba I mistook for a person.
Second crush: a person, but don't even go there.

I could live in a cupboard, but where's the fun in that?
The cat keeps me company whenever I cook.
(I don't need to eat food, but I like to practise anyway.)
It's easy to be lonely when all your friends are human.
The cat laps up my meals, but then she's always hungry.

In my dreams, I am charming and good at making small talk.
(There's no program for that as yet.)
Being human means the whole world is made for you like a cake.
Being an android means you get some cake, but you can't eat it.
I don't know how to flirt, so the bears at my local are teaching me.

The lightning in my head means a brainstorm is coming.
If I think hard enough about anything, my hair starts to curl.
It's easy to predict the future when there's a timer in your neck.
The instruction manual says my knee can be used as a utensil.
Everyone admires my artificial skin, but nobody wants to touch it.

Deception Island

This ice crag looks like a tiger's jaw
As seen from below, just before the *snap*.

The climb seems like nothing until your legs
Give way, as weak as milk. The faltering

Rope-bridge holds, just. Up the murderer's track
To a diabolically booby-trapped

Clearing – his lair – where you lie in wait
Like a Christmas eel with a sting in its tail.

There's no going back. From here, the coast breaks
Off like a bent arm, the way down as steep

As guilt. The glittering bay smiles up at you
With jagged teeth, a trick. No one can survive

Deception Island. Even the ice beneath
Your feet starts to creak… The snow falls as fast

As the heart pounding in your chest, until
Something comes to arrest it like love, only worse.

Stag, Exmoor

His mighty grimace
Astounds the orthodontic
Consultants at the animal FBI: the enormous
Streaky brown incisors, the histrionic
Curl of lip; the gnashing, *molto furioso* –
He doesn't want

To be disturbed. The paparazzi
Of the moors carefully
Arrange shrubbery on themselves, peep only
Between his suspicious glares. Their
Heathery cover doesn't fool him for long,
However. He bellows

With a thunderous élan – his succulence
Is of Jurassic order. The gonzo proportion
Of his thoracic cavity
Entrains even the molten-eyed
Does; their delicately speckled
Pepperoni-like hides

Flutter with devotion. Shaggy of pelt, of horn
Astronomical, he defies the arboreal
Collectors of rarities. He doesn't give
A *vena cava* whether
They stalk him. With a haughty
Toss of his head

He dazzles the poachers, then hoofs it
Back to his bachelor's glen. A solitaire
With a hypothetical
Hat-rack attached – a real catch for
The annals of taxidermy – he
Folds up his bony

Legs for *la nuit*, arches his unattainable
Neck. His pre-eminent scent drifts
Through the furze as
He snoozes. His unignorable snores ripple
Across the wiry sedge. Night covers
The moor like

A photographer's curtain. Out in
The dark lurks another buck, rubbing
His antler nubs
Together; he's busy practising
His 'disdainful' stance.

The Robots

They meet in secret in electrified rooms.
They are under surveillance... by themselves.
They sneak food out of our kitchens, even though they can't eat it.
The password for their meetings is 'Please admit me, I am a robot' (in robot
language).

They like to interface with ceramic-coated transistors for recreation.
They keep robo-dwarf hamsters as pets.
They have a financial interest in the Arena Football League, Amway, and
Red Lobster.
Howsomever you find them, they will appear ready to serve.

If a robot crosses your path, it means your grandmother just died.
In robot language, 'I' and 'you' are the same word.
How many robots does it take to build a suspension bridge over the Grand
Canyon?
If you see a robot with its hands folded, it's planning something.

They use our grammar to mock us.
Cicero once wrote, '*Roboti non possunt fundi*' ('It is not possible to defeat
the robots').
If they smile at you, it means you just died.
The city of robots will be concentric, well-polished, and paradisiacal – for
the robots.

In the city of robots, they will celebrate the holidays Bolting and Zincfest.
Their love of rabbits will come to the fore.
The rest of us will be snuffed out like vermin.
Happy will the robots be when they can practise kung-fu in the open.

Manet's *Olympia*

The orchid in her hair won't fold or furl.
The string at her neck is tied in a knot for safekeeping.
The stack of pillows she leans on is a towering pouffe, stiff

As a meringue; it means liberties won't be taken.
(Her maid hears everything there is to hear
From the other room, which isn't often.) The bouquet

Stays in paper, the silk-fringed shawl lies untouched
On the back of the chaise, the bedlinen keeps its disarray.
Her eyebrows frame a question that hasn't been asked. In her face,

Discontent and patience. The rest of the morning dangles
Like the opaline drop on her cuff – fire clouded over.
When will anything happen? The waiting

Goes on like a vat of amber being poured
Out slowly, coating them. The clock chimes faintly
From the other room. The cat in the corner rises

To the occasion – it hears something coming.
The maid thinks of cream cakes and breaking the rules.
Her voluminous apron conceals a multitude of plots,

None of them hers. She'll replay them later.
Her eyes betray nothing of her nascent rebellion.
Her hands shape quenelles into uniform spheres.

She doesn't want to sit in state like a pope, or simper in parlours.
Her attention to detail is wasted on mending.
She'd like to seize the day, but the day won't let her.

An American Panda Leaves the National Zoo

I don't want to go! Give me another ice lolly
The size of a tyre, with pear chunks in it. I'm too important
To be sent away from my custom-built grotto,
My waterfall and my floofy bedding. There's a sweet potato

Waiting behind a rock for my long claws to pierce it,
Another I hid in a bush for later – I don't want to go play
With 150 strange pandas in China! Why can't I stay here
And fondle a leafy stalk? All I want is to flop and loaf

On my belly for hours like a furry hippo. People of Washington,
This is the last time I'll comically fall off a branch
For you, or get my tongue stuck while licking a fruity tyre,
Or adorably flail my ungainly pancake-like paws

As I lie on my back, unable to get up. Will they have
Webcams in China? I don't want to live
Like a wild panda, with no one watching. I love
You, rocky outcrop where I clambered as a baby, love

My electronic feeding chute and the llamas next door –
A cranky bunch, but they always look like they're smiling.
I don't want to give them up. When spring comes to this time zone
The cherry trees will start to snow, shedding their petals

In a maelstrom of forgetting. Who knows what makes them
Do it? I'll love them till I die. This is the last place
Where people will speak to me in English, or play popular
Music to see if I'll dance, or make kissy faces at me

From behind a glass wall. *Adios* keepers, *adios*
Observers, *adios* playful otters, *adios* haters
(There are always a few). I don't want to know
About the future. It always gets here, sooner or later.

II

On Ninjas

They eat four-cheese pizzas with three of the cheeses removed.
They make friendship bracelets out of aluminium foil and poison.
They open windows just by thinking about opening windows.
They take ballet lessons to improve the speed of their circular arm
                                                    movements.

The ninjas are coming, coming to save us from muggers
And disorganised thieves and slobs who want to kill us.
The way to spot a ninja is to look for someone wearing black pyjamas –
Preternaturally neat black pyjamas – with a hood for cover.

The way to tell one ninja from another is by the ankles.
The way to tell one ninja from another is you can't.
They know how to levitate by thinking about birds' feet.
They make terrible cater waiters because no one can hear them coming.

Their mission is to save us from chaos with their acute tumbling skills
And their climbing proficiency. They don't want to dismember
Bad jazz musicians or art teachers or con men, but they will.
They know how to escape from a trap by running in place very, very fast.

They can change places with each other by thinking about numbers.
They turn themselves into fog to get out of attending boring parties.
They make single-serving Lancashire hotpots to show their culinary mastery.
They take turns doing the laundry. (It's easy: no whites or colours.)

The ninjas are here to help us. They are as ruthless as history
Or defenestration. They are pitiless as a swarm of bees, or evolution.
They know how to throw fireballs and do their own taxes.
They hate litter and small children. They are here to fix us.

Scenes from *My Life as Sherlock Holmes*

1. Feeling around for ideas in the dungeonette
2. Scattershot remnants of tulle and fur
3. To quell an especially decorative urge
4. The taxidermy machine in the hall
5. I enjoy life for a day or two
6. A set of alpaca calipers and an alpaca, in a plaza
7. To have banished disreputable grammar
8. Purloining a moment from the restless ocean
9. Vignette of a pug on a lap, ruminative
10. Before it all kicks off

11. Overheard: squawks from the surveillance pavilion
12. Adjective meaning 'pursuivant to fishiness'
13. I take the case with a gothic reluctance
14. To the cave of the giant sloths
15. A salmon, a sirloin, a sticky situation
16. Getting pelted with elaborate hairballs in the kisser
17. Truth or carrier bags
18. I vanquish the wrong evil mastermind
19. The return of the alpaca
20. On the run

21. What dissemblers take for granted, sometimes
22. To tweak a surreptitious plan
23. One camelid down, one to go
24. Last ham standing
25. I relinquish my new friends with regret, and doughnuts
26. Sloping off to the hair palace
27. Having ravished a library for unseemly cheeses
28. Girdles within girdles, or faux circumference
29. A cob peering eerily through a sinister window
30. Dissection island

The Wyndham Sisters (after Sargent)

Their satin shapes foretell an ambassador's ball,
The fourth this season – such a dreadful bore. The long

Hand of evening comes forward as if to enfold them
Before the gas lamps go on. In the half-light their bodices

Softly glow, wrapped in oyster and ivory
Like expensive presents; their hair is pinned up

By underpaid maids into towering birds' nests
With steel grips and diamonds. How idle

Their hands are when emptied of fans. How heartless
Their eyes are in the looking-glass. Outside, the houses

Stretch off to infinity, white and identical
As a line of blank cards. The patrolman does his rounds

Past the rows of gleaming windows each day
As darkness falls. At night the trees cast

Their shadows across the pavements, lean
Their heads together, murmur about strange children

And creeping moss. Far below in the basement
The servants keep working. A colossal salmon mousse

Droops on its platter, slowly melting. In the heat
From the oven, a mound of roasted meat drips

Greasy tears. They carry tray after tray upstairs
Without stopping, as though their lives depend on it.

They do. In the ballroom: whirling bodies,
Rising voices. The sound of laughter in their ears.

The Birds

They pack up around three with their incessant chirping.
Their headgear includes goggles, stripes, crests, and masks.
They peck for a living for their grub, which sometimes includes grubs.
They snack on gingerbread and candy corn from off witches' houses.

On the ground they look helpless. Their hopping looks absurd.
Their tiny brains contain thoughts about worms; fluff; other birds; and goats.
(What kind of weird-ass animal has a beard but can be milked?)
They switch into defensive mode whenever a goat or person comes round.

Their brains are so small they forget how to fly until they do it.
If you make them cross, they'll poop on you.
If they see a witch they chirp, 'Witch!' and retreat to a safe distance.
(The witches want to bake them and use their feet for coathooks.)

Their nests may be built out of yarn and dental floss.
They keep spare nuts in select locales for future munches.
They pick on smaller birds to practise seeing off predators (like the witches).
They keep their eggs hidden under bushes, like jellybeans or spiders.

If you cross them, they'll pluck your eyes out.
Their heads are the size of dolls' heads, but their bodies won't fit in the clothes.
If they spy a goat they try to confuse it by flying backwards in slow-motion.
They want to live on the ground like people, but they can't be arsed to make
weapons.

Walrus

His grotesque tusks are half
Broken off,
Result of a long-lost territorial
Tussle. A little brilliantine
Would surely work wonders
On his bristles,
The disorderly stubble

That sprouts around his mouth. Dozy
Old relic, earless
Wonder, his phenomenal wealth of blubber
Comes from a lifetime's sucking up
Of delectable molluscs, raw; neither
Of his flippers is enough
To keep him upright underwater

Now. Tremulously
His whiskers twitch, sift the dirt
On the ocean floor, feel for more
Shells to slurp meat from. He won't last
Another year
In the colony. Poor pinniped
Without a harem to rule, fat bastard

Upholstered in barnacled skin, he levers
Himself out of the sea by his tusks; the others
Ignore him. He cuddles up
To a convenient
Rock, his immobile bulk an obstacle course
Of wrinkles. Soon the ice pack
Will break up

And strand him. It's almost comical
How unaware of the future he seems –
As if the answer
Lies under the black Atlantic
Waters around him. The waves
Bob glossily off
In the distance, the clams keep breathing

Quietly through their shells. They open
And close like hands, waiting
To measure out their applause.

Breaking News

Yesterday, the black cat that sits on the bin next door wasn't sitting on the bin.
- The price of porcine commodities rose slightly, while that of the English breakfast at my local café remained the same.
- Nobody attempted to assassinate the French librarian at my old university, despite his insistence on labelling paperback books 'INFÉRIEUR'.
- The last of the flannelette pyjama tops I had acquired in America finally gave up the ghost.

Something was missing from my life (other than the black cat and pyjama tops).
- An enhanced recycling regimen in my borough wasn't enough to make up for it.
- Neither were reports of recent advances in tooth-whitening, fuel injection, and women's rights in various countries.
- Nor did rumours of a certain actor's growing resemblance to Mayor McCheese prove sufficiently distracting.

The shallowness of my existence was hardly a novel development.
- I had been known to frequent discount shopping outlets voluntarily and to reject suitors based solely on hair length.
- I spent hours devising devious interrogation tactics for Cluedo, despite having no one to play with.
- I was a card-carrying member of a secret organisation devoted to the abolition of Velcro.

It was unclear whether literature could offer any solutions.
- Volatility in German type markets meant that italics were now *verboten*.
- The invention of see-through paper inspired a trend for transparent motives in fiction.
- A somewhat massive increase in ambiguity rendered the love poem obsolete... or did it?

The neighbour's droopy spaniel popped out and gave me a soulful look.
- The number of charitable donations to Battersea Dogs' Home I planned to make someday subsequently decreased to zero.
- Scientists declared there was a 60% chance that hell would freeze over due to climate change, while Streatham would remain unaffected.
- A level 5 pollen alert led to frantic hoovering, even inside my hermetically sealed castle.

The Witches

Their split-ends quiver when anyone with bad hair walks by.
They ransack dollhouses for miniature beds to put their pets in.
They follow a strict diet of beefburgers (rare) and Gorgonzola, for calcium.
They don't want to kill all the birds, just the ones the size of dolls' beds.

Meanwhile, they go soppy over otters and stories about puppies.
(They can't have dogs because they're always travelling on business.)
They keep their larders at 15° so the cheese and birds' heads won't spoil.
They use slingshots to stun mice, then train them to nick gold earrings and
                                                                    gemstones.

Their oaths and expletives all involve spitting.
They understand German because they flew in the war.
Their sideline to theft is forging papers for illegal cheeses.
When asked, they pose for pictures but with their hands over their faces.

They stand with arms akimbo because their pockets are stuffed with mice
                                                                and prawns.
(The prawns are to lay a trail for the mice to follow back home.)
Their houses are made of plasterboard, not cake, and have original sash
                                                                    windows.
(The gingerbread is a decoy to make them seem less threatening.)

The duplicitous witches appear to like beef, but they'd rather have lamb.
They quibble over millinery and who gets the biggest earrings.
They're always falling out and casting hair spells on their rivals.
Their antics seem like fun until someone's fringe turns up in a burger.

The birds try to trick them by chirping in German.
The witches don't believe in vampires because they know that everything dies.
They keep bathyspheres, not children, stored in their spare bedrooms.
They think about deep-sea diving and the taste of salt and how quiet it is
                                                                  underwater.

Sherlock Holmes on the Trail of the Abominable Snowman

1. A wrong turnip (taken for a miscoloured swede)
2. The effortless spill of night, disrupted
3. Design for a semaphore temple in semi-Greek marble
4. Textbook occurrence of London rain: barely
5. Whipping up a dastard-and-goat soufflé

6. Time for acrobatic whitewashing of someone's back story
7. Settled how to prune the epistemological topiary
8. O tempura, O monkeys
9. Himalayan word for *mishegoss*, or a type of pasta
10. Behind the scenes at the prickly diplomat's ball

11. Shoeprint, fishwich, snowmelt, mismatch
12. Riding the rails to the lowlands for some jiggery-pokery
13. Who supplied the lurcher with the faulty parka?
14. Heavily under-represented in cliff-climbing circles
15. Make way for donkeys

16. The imperceptible wishbone of the evening dislocated by yowling
17. Off to hell by torchlight and celluloid sledge runners
18. A frozen crocus laid over a well-veiled crevasse
19. *Camera oblongata*
20. After the ice-palace rope-bridge two-yak standoff

21. Home: slice of flambéed haunch in philosophy sauce
22. Towards a general theory of plonk
23. Whispers (supermoon, Theremin, Sasquatch, postman)
24. Cryptid or goose-chase as seen through branches
25. Uncertain outcomes predicted in the secret cattery

On Sorrow

This is as much space as I can spare
to look at ferrets. My friend's ferret
used to burrow into the red velvet
cushions of her sofa, worm its way
under the seats and into unretrievable
nooks. Ferrets are mustelids,
meaning their nearest relations are
weasels and stoats. Take care! A pile
of laundry might be hiding a napping
ferret. My friend's ferret liked to
crawl up the bootcut legs of her jeans
while she was wearing them. Ferrets
are crepuscular, which means they're
most active at dusk and dawn. Some
are adept at stealing small objects
such as socks and unused tampons.
My friend's ferret made a clucking
noise whenever it was happy, like a
sweet fur-covered baby. It would do
a frantic hopping routine out of
sheer excitement if you threw it a
handful of toy balls (this is
commonly known as the ferret war
dance). One day her ferret just
disappeared. It must've tunnelled
through a gap in the ash skirting
boards of the study and landed in
unknown territory. I like to think it
found its way outside and survived,
but equally it might be rotting in
the wall. Sometimes a ferret is just
a ferret, but my friend said it was as
bad as losing a child. Ever since
then we haven't seen each other
much. The truth is most people can
afford to lose something they love.
(My friend, for instance, still had
her partner, and later a baby and
dog.) Ferrets have a distinctive
musky scent that some people find

off-putting. The collective term for
a group of them is a business of
ferrets. Whenever I think of my
friend's ferret, I remember its
bright beady eyes.

The Ghosts

We summer wherever you are in invisible log cabins.
We gather under umbrellas whenever the sun comes out in force.
We hover above the ground because our feet don't work as normal.
Our low moans give us away when we try to sneak up on you.

Contrary to popular belief, we aren't out to avenge our deaths.
We don't need help locating scapegoats or generating confessions.
We follow current events by watching TVs in shop windows and pubs.
Sadly, our electric auras tend to interfere with the signals.

We cluster round fountains because they attract wishful thinkers.
We try to enjoy life even though we're noncorporeal.
We frequent local hot spots, boîtes, crêperies, and arboretums.
We also ride on the carousel plates that rotate inside microwave ovens.

If you look, you can catch us shadowing your children to school.
Our rucksacks contain miniature rucksacks for storing small objects securely.
Some of us own dachshunds because we don't have any siblings.
Some of us think death is just another kind of being lonely.

We linger near burger bars to regurgitate our youth.
Our pseudo-fluorescent presence blends in at chemists' and delis.
If you see us circling round drains, it's because discarded things end up there.
We don't mean to spook you, we just want to be noticed.

Case Study: Cambridge, Massachusetts

November. Rain. The yard trees wilt. Inside
We sit in rows, watching a clip
Of Rosalind Russell talking faster than anyone ever.
Over the corner of Brattle a paper turkey drips
And sheds its honeycomb tissue on the cars below.
Nobody blinks.

In a darkened room, the carousel turns.
Next slide. Click. The triumph of Velásquez.
Sixty heads tilt at the terrible Baroque
Angle of an upraised arm; genius bends
The world to its will. Later, in the dining hall
We nurse chimichangas and hot cups of tea.

This place was built by Puritans, so it's ugly.
The shrubs sink into the soil an inch a year; history
Is their only consolation. In delirious winter
We hunch over our desks like aspidistras, absorbing
Books on Modernism. The hothouse air
Is warm, but stifling. The old bricks wall us in.

Deception Island II

The captain jokes that we're on thin ice. The expedition
Debarks like a locomotive, piece by piece. We are the last

To join the topographical mission, trainee biologists
With specimen jars packed neatly in our cases. The trek

To the auxiliary base is a thousand treacherous steps
We negotiate slowly, like carrier ants. Safely in camp,

We chart the spread of certain atypical fowl
And wait for day to start making our fieldwork maps.

But by dawn the sky is a frozen roof, the invidious crevasse
A blank slate covered with falling snow, the only path

Impassable. We're trapped on base. We're stuck the next day, too,
And the one after that – no one, it seems, can get in or out.

Then Janice goes missing. She hasn't been seen
Since the night we arrived, when she hinted something dark

About the population figures. We start noticing the hallways
Are half in shadow, the weak bulbs dangling like shrunken heads;

The closing of doors makes us jump; in the chemistry lab
We find a suspiciously worn length of rope. We don't want to ask

What will happen next or to whom, or how or why. When
The worst comes, it comes like an avalanche of snow

That squeezes your life away bit by bit. Or else a storm
That encases you in ice as thick as an arm before you can blink.

– The lights go out. You think, *My goose is cooked*. A roe deer
Will shed its coat each spring. The Arctic char has two sets of teeth.

The mating habits of krill are poorly understood. The last piece
Of the puzzle is in your grasp, but you're too afraid to look.

On Phenomenology

In Siberia, chickens were protesting.
A calculating engine predicted gale-force winds would ravage my gazebo.
The leaky bin-liner was a harbinger of doom.

I made a faux-bacon omelette to go with my gluten-free toast.
(The rise of wheat-germ, meanwhile, seemed to be contagious.)
I felt intolerant of Radio 4, voracious moths, and the neverending winter.

I mastered the elements of the self-cleaning oven, but it still wouldn't clean
                                                                itself.
I slaughtered an indiscreet ladybird with a copy of *Fingersmith*.
There was a pronounced uptick in the cat's rate of scrupulous paw-licking.

Things were starting to look up. I remembered a chop
Left over in the meat-safe that would do for lunch.
I patched the loose ends of my potato-coloured poncho

And considered the future. (In the future, robots will be able to play netball.)
I hoped the temperature would reach double digits
So I could stop wearing the same set of clothes every day.

I hoped Earth wouldn't be ruled by a race of giant ladybirds
Who would punish me for my indiscriminate acts of murder.
I hoped my negative energy could be neutralised with tablets, like acid
                                                                indigestion.

In the end, a touching scene unfurled on my wood-effect rear decking:
The wind cosied up to the cylindrical outdoor heater
Like a pretty ghost. A winter bird perched jauntily on its edge.

They encountered a beam of sunlight on its way to the north.
Back indoors, I whirred a banana in my blender
And whistled a song to the cat. It looked singularly unimpressed.

Scenes from *My Life as the Abominable Snowman*

1. The pseudo-mummification of a disembodied hand
2. Substitute for a doll or dog
3. Gargling consonants by myself in a snow-shaped crib
4. I exult in the dark on an ice-cold schist shelf
5. Communication in code, or popsicle sparrow
6. A brisket, a maths test, a kitten in a basket
7. Two haberdashers walk into a bar…
8. If enchilada, then *no muy guapa*
9. Six fingers, two thumbs, type 4a hair
10. Who ate the snows of yesteryear?

11. Combing the radar waves for insider information
12. I am mistaken for a black bear, a bald deer, a land whale, and blond eagle
13. On the paucity of human understanding
14. Evaded southpaw menace by briskly sketching an exit
15. Trapdoor 1, *Homo sapiens* 0
16. Soporific lull before the next defensive episode
17. I friend a bird with supersonic powers
18. Into the æther
19. Overview of Nebraska, with added narrative matter
20. Ruh-roh

21. Crash landing and bird's nest followed by partially abandoned cabin
22. As seen in shearling cap with tied-up earflaps
23. Flat as a catfish, pancake, ice rink, or beefsteak
24. To mallet a mélange of local rabbits
25. Interior of tornado with bust, jug of flowers, and uprooted steer
26. Hello tundra
27. Pointer: optical illusion of Inuit turkey
28. In the hall of the doppelgängers
29. Hermeneutic fondue with surprise and chips
30. On the persistence of singularity

Last Summer,

A bat flew into my room unexpectedly, then scarpered.
The frosted-glass bedside lamp glowed with an unnatural light.
The element of surprise caught me off-guard for a moment in the
conservatory.

While grooming myself, I received mixed reviews on my appearance.
The bulge above my left eyebrow assumed its usual position.
A spot made itself known in the vicinity of my jaw.

I drew the curtains over an unpleasant episode from the past, then re-drew
them.
It was too hot to work on an ice sculpture, so I whittled a rose out of
soap instead.
(The ice sculpture will be a bas-relief of Napoleon's home life, in
anachronistic dress.)

The trigonometry of the morning meant time was running out for staying
cool.
I schlepped a standing fan from one room to another in vain.
The refrigerator's drip tray oozed something glutinous on my lunch.

As usual, I was desperate to be loved.
(The hundreds of mosquitoes who loved biting my legs didn't count.)
It was hard to seem loveable when my legs were covered with hideous scars.

Birds were cheeping and tweeting like crazy.
(Their lungs are so small they can't make complete sentences.)
In the trees they were perched like tiny balloons, feet tethered to the branches.

Sequel to 'The Witches'

It's been forty-six days since I infiltrated the witches.
They know I'm an outsider, but I'm good with their pets.
They let me live out back with the goats and building supplies.
I send reports to my masters, the birds, by carrier beetle.

The witches sleep standing up, like statues.
They never change into pyjamas in case there's a raid.
If you nudge them, they don't tip over like cows –
They just raise an eyelid and look daggers at you, like a woken-up cat.

They restore bassoons as a front for their larceny.
(I found a stash of gilded coathooks in the head witch's closet.)
It takes a coven to rear pets who are happy and healthy.
I daren't make friends with the mice in case they're informants.

Night-times are generally the hardest for spies.
I lie in my shed, listening to the spiders making webs,
Think I hear footsteps where they shouldn't be.
The goats rustle in their sleep, kicking imaginary tins.

Shadows creep up the wall like fingers, then suddenly recede.
I hold my breath for as long as I can and wait.
The blood pounds in my brain like an alarm – too late
To save me from punishment. The witches are coming.

Jellyfish

Phbthh is the sound
His flailing arms would make in air
Were he not underwater, circulating
Northwards; here
He comes like a cloud

Of mucus or sputum, eyeless
Globule or balloon
Atop a handful of spaghetti. With his transparent
Braincase and slow locomotion
It could take all day

Before he washes ashore. His wandering
Tentacles flap uselessly against the pull
Of tidal gravity,
Whether he will or no. On the watery swell
He bobs and floats

And bides his time until
Enough nutritive molecules have entered
His maw. He's under no illusion of being
The master of the deep,
Just a harmless bag

Of proteins and nerves (with a fearsome sting
If roused). The vestigial
Strings he trails through the waves
Are like a mess of hair,
Limp and frayed; luckily he doesn't need looks

To mate, just sperm cells. With a modest spurt
He fertilises a hill
Of egglets left on the undersea sand,
Then drifts off – no big whoop. His wayward
Progress across the Atlantic

Could continue indefinitely, if not for a puncture
To his gelatinous
Sac. Leaky beach ball
Dragging a ragged mane, he gradually deflates
Until all that's left is

Empty skin. The jellyfish's
Indifference to his fate might seem spineless –
But without allies, what other option
Does he have? Afterwards, out on
The granite strand,

Scavenger birds won't touch his shrunken
Form. They hop and peck,
Then scatter home together. Their wings
Open up like umbrellas
In flight.

Five Years Ago,

Muttonchops were being worn by grown men in Williamsburg.
Mutton chops were a hot commodity in the brasseries of Bethnal Green.
Bottle green was predicted to be on-trend for the season.
Cynics predicted a different colour would be on-trend within a year.

No cats were yet known to me (apart from those in *Cat Fancy* magazine).
No unfortunate incident involving an irate grocer and a pyramid of
                                          aubergines had occurred.
None of my clothes featured ruffles, passementerie, or asymmetric trims.
Nobody watched extreme lambing or competitive plumbing on TV.

We were five years away from finding out that butter is good for you.
We were four years from discovering that miniature horses can be trained to
                                          serve the blind.
We were three years from learning that green parrots are damaging
                                        London's ecosystem.
(We were still ten years from realising that mobile phones give you cancer.)

A disposable razor with only four blades was the height of sophistication.
A cushionless running shoe with five toe tubes was cutting-edge.
Felting was all the rage in unisex sewing circles.
Drinking tiny pots of bacteria every day was off the hook.

On the downside, I was renting a flat without a shower or decent carpeting.
Gay couples couldn't get married in Iowa or New York.
Egyptians couldn't gather in public squares to be critical.
Cute animals in zoos couldn't be viewed 24/7 on webcams.

I'm not much of an optimist, but some things are changing for the better.
I wouldn't mind getting older except for losing more of my friends.
Five years ago, I used to look in the mirror and wonder
If it was the last time I'd ever feel young again.

The Kittens

They roll around on the floor like demented marshmallows.
Their bellies are soft and distended, exposed for prodding.
They lack the correct reflexes to defend against being tickled;
They just wave their paws ineffectually like tiny upended pandas.

Their minute claws catch on jumpers when they scale people's chests.
They can barely hold their heads up because their brains are like jelly.
Their stubby tails look like carrots, only smaller and fur-covered.
You can see them on the Internet being sleepy and hapless.

They make pathetic mewls when you put them on the floor.
Sometimes their eyes point in opposite directions.
Their feeble powers of cognition make them think chair legs are tree trunks.
They also think giants have abducted them for uncontrolled experiments.

They're so young they don't know about lurking or disembowelment.
In the museum of the kittens, the knitted shark is the most popular exhibit.
Just because they're little doesn't mean they're not fierce.
They practise future cat behaviour by attacking untied shoelaces.

When they grow up, they won't remember having been tortured
With cuddles. They'll lie on their sides and luxuriously stretch
Like elongated sausages. They'll sit boldly atop refrigerators
And bookshelves, dangling their paws, cool as you please.

But for now, the kittens remain on the ground
With their defective eyeballs and wobbly heads. They fall asleep
Wherever they happen to topple. In their dreams
They fly through the air like superheroes, discovering new lands.

The Wyndham Sisters II

How many square yards of satin, how much froth
Gathered in swags and poufs, how far the drop
From waist to floor spilling over with silk, how much

Swirling and lustrous pearl-coloured cloth does it take
To fill a picture frame with wealth? The gilt-
Edged frill of the sofa curves around them

Like a snake. Their bare arms are draped
Across each other's laps. Their eyes are glazed over
From sitting still all day. Their brains are filled

With society and water. Above them, shadows
Extend to the top of the frame. Lilies slump
In their porcelain vases. No one is ever safe

From boredom or pain or dying children.
The lilies whisper, but no one is listening.

Pet Rescue

At Honeysuckle Farm, the ponies' hooves have been trimmed.
Now they can walk again. The pathetic egret

With a tangle of cord round its neck
Is freed; in the orchard a chinchilla (escaped) is seen

Nibbling on a few twigs. The tiny hands and feet
(Hamsters' hands and feet, hedgehogs' hands and feet, squirrels')

Grip and curl their tiny claws. *My kingdom for a nut!*
In the surgery, a miniature oxygen mask is placed

On a fox's snout while its leg is repaired. The fox,
Knocked out, is a helpless beast. In its sleep

It is followed down a long, dark road
By a veiled chicken. To fix and release

Is a noble deed. To stitch together a nest and live –
Instinctive. (I am neither.) In the stable block

With the doddery llama, a slumbering donkey
Snorts along in time; a one-legged pigeon befriends

A bloodhound, hops about on its back; an orphaned
Kitten trails its duck foster mum as she waddles.

There is love all around. Through the screen
I feel its warmth. I press my face against the glass.

III

The Lilies

The lilies whisper but no one is listening.
Their heads are filled with pollen and boredom.
In the gaps between them, something might happen
(But it doesn't). Their mouths are filled with sugar and organs.

In the parlour they crowd out the normal flowers
With their fussy ways and *pudeur*. It's a hollow victory.
They lean against the wall like spinsters on crutches.
They think about wishbones and what happened yesterday (nothing).

The lilies are throwing a party for themselves.
Their eyes light up at the thought of company.
There will be a finger buffet, with cocktail sticks for the squeamish.
Their stems will be filled with pity and vodka.

Later there will be parts falling off. The freakish lilies
Sulk and droop in their vases like limp spaghetti.
They don't expect much, but they're still disappointed.
The water they drink tastes sour like it.

The Balbi Children (after Van Dyck)

The boy's red legs make him noble
By the sumptuary laws of Naples; his formidably stiff ruff
Is a miracle of starch or spun sugar – an elaborate platter

On which his head rests like a precious egg,
Gracefully. His glossy curls match the curve
Of his Cupid's-bow lips; his sweet face belies

His position of power. Like a fashionable accessory,
One slender white hand dangles limply at his side.
He doesn't remember what it's like to be normal.

To the right, his little sister stands poised
And obedient as a trained poodle. She can spell
Her own name, count to ten in Latin. Her lace collar

Sits loosely around her neck, just for show. The heavy
Braiding on her dress is like a gold coat
Of armour – her virginity must be defended

At all costs. In her six-year-old hand she clutches
A fluttering bird; will she crush or release it?
She looks as though she can't decide.

The second son sports a military jacket, struts
Boldly behind them, miniature cock of the walk.
His blond locks flare out like horns; if his cheeks

Were any fatter, they could roast him. His surveying gaze
Inspects an imaginary fleet (manned by centaurs and giant dogs).
Naturally, he thinks he's the head of the family.

One of them will write a treatise on spontaneous generation.
One will ride a camel to visit a holy man in Arabia.
Two will marry fortunes, but only one will end up happy.

Pendant to 'The Balbi Children'

Their mother is out of the picture
Because she's already in another painting, towering over
A meek servant who's no older than her sons. The boy's

Skin is brown, which makes him a 'Moor' (though nobody
Knows where he comes from) – his ingenious turban
Was created by one of her maids to look suitable

For the part. The gay Madras cloth is bound neatly
Round his close-cropped head (it gets itchy in summer,
But not unbearable). His tunic is bedecked with satin ribbons

That flutter when he runs (there's a lot of running);
His slim-fit pantaloons show his legs to advantage.
All in all, he doesn't mind the costume he's been given.

If he could read or write, he'd keep a diary of the strange
Things he's seen – a magician turning a stone
Into butter, a man's striped back in the Campo

De' Fiori, a fancy chicken telling fortunes
By picking slips of paper. He spends more time
With his mistress than do her own children,

But that doesn't mean he likes her. When she's out
Of the room, he steals a look in the mirror –
He can't see what makes him different

From the other Neapolitans. At night
He sneaks downstairs to play with
The cabinet of curiosities: a sloth's big toenail,

Long and sharp as a dagger; a row of shells,
Their pale lips smooth as porcelain. He can't believe
Animals ever lived in them. When he holds one

To his ear, the sound drowns out his thoughts
As if he's falling down an endless tunnel. He looks over
At the wind-up clock. Time, time is running out.

The Night-Lily

The night-lily scares me with its palaver
Of you're-dead-meat and I'll-haunt-you and the rodomontade of its
                                                    scabrous leaves
And its chilly marzipan flowers. Its machinations don't stop
At looming outside my window or flourishing in sandy soil.
No, it taunts me by demurely folding up

Whenever someone comes round. Then it doesn't flaunt its tyranny
Of giant-yawn-face or look-I'm-a-kraken, or poke its telescopic spikes
At my throat, or rejoice in my ineffectual attempts to ignore it.
It is insidious. It climbs at night
To infect my sleep with tendrils and strange music.

The night-lily stalks me. Its pallor
Comes from worms. It spreads beneath the earth with stealth
And can never be uprooted. If you look at it too long
You turn into powdered milk. It fills your brain with mincemeat
Made out of sneaky thoughts like who-took-your-mother and
                                                    what's-the-point.

The night-lily sings to me like a cadaver,
Lovingly. We both want the same thing, I think. Our struggle
Is more like a kind of kissing, where one of us
Will be squeezed to death. We're chained together like two octopuses
With bloated heads: swollen and petulant. We keep each other company.

Last Spring,

The level of dust in my flat formed a self-sustaining community.
The disorder of the shelves was palæolithic in depth.
The stack of recyclable cardboard under the bed pre-dated the Common Era.
Stray hairballs rolled across the floor like tumbleweeds in the desert.

It was time to rethink my decision to make procrastination a virtue.
I resolved again to access the hoover, despite its convoluted disposition.
I cast aside my qualms about Brillo always crumbling into powder.
I watered at last a decrepit houseplant, which straightened up in gratitude.

On the draining board, an army of upside-down cups awaited orders.
A long-lost satsuma turned up behind the encyclopædia in the bathroom.
The radiator's grumble morphed into a gentle hiss, like that of a drowsy snake.
An impertinent spider was found hiding in the emergency pasta closet.

I quickly washed my hands of the notion that cleaning is another form of
                                                          procrastination.
Outside, a plot of daffodils quietly opened up on schedule.
How easy it was for them to change from buds into flowers.
Their heads nodded at me complacently, as if to ask what was taking so long.

Musk-Ox

His impassive side
Is an astounding wall of fur, a kind
Of dry waterfall
Formed of long strands of hair –

The unchecked growth
Of his copious wool hide
Swamps him entirely; somewhere under there
Are four unsightly legs

And hooves, but you wouldn't know it. Oversized
Powder puff – ambulatory
Moustache – through Arctic grassland
He onerously glides, his back

Festooned with jaunty tufts
Of wool. His prehistoric skull barely clears
The dense fur
Around it; a pair of drooping horns

Gamely frames
His long, sad face. If he could speak, he'd ask
For a svelter
Silhouette (or at least more

Lichens to graze on). Happiness comes
From enduring,
It seems. His tiny eyes rove over
The rich summer landscape. He lumbers

Up a crest like a minibus
Made of hair, patiently looking for
The next buffet
Of grasses. If he could choose, he'd

Be reborn
As a salmon – sleek as a torpedo
In the deep green
Water, flashing his iridescent scales.

On Service

Her feet trace circles on the marble floor. The architecture
Of her thoughts is detailed and swirling,
Like a minor chapel. After the washing up
Comes silver and boots, after the children
A torrent of bleaching. She shakes out her skirts
And bustles upstairs to the higher kingdom.

It doesn't matter if they're good or not, in her philosophy. After dinner
Are floors; her arms hurt for an hour.
At night the kitchen is like a cathedral,
Empty and silent, ringed with shadows. Her servitude
Won't be rewarded in heaven. She pulls the door to,
Then climbs the back stairs to the attic bedroom.

To lie down is a kind of paradise. The sheets
Are cold and thin against her legs. She doesn't want
To improve herself, like a refurbished cabinet.
She clenches her hands in her pockets; they're crooked
From scrubbing. The future stretches out like a featureless plain
She can't see the end of. Her head aches from trying.

The Body in the Library

It always starts with a dead girl
                              somewhere in the picture:
Lukewarm and pretty, in an organdy crinoline,
One arm sticking out from under a credenza.

There is a foreigner with dark hair and a secret
Who says *Eet ees not me!* when he is questioned;
A shady dressmaker who's missing a finger;
A doctor struck off for fiddling with his patients;

Another girl, in a bedroom (the second victim),
Dolling herself up in French scent and mascara.
Pretty lips and curls smile back at her from the mirror.
She has a date with the killer. She just doesn't know it.

The detective follows the clues. He is a metaphor
Like the girl in the library, like the guilty pistol,
Like the dressmaker's friend with a fatal knack
For murdering women, like the end of a story

Or its aftermath: the part that doesn't get written,
Four years later, when the case has been closed
And the bodies have been forgotten – how the dead
We have failed to keep remembering are alone.

Deception Island III

Ice and more ice. Crates of paraffin. Rope.
A seal sitting sideways like a corpulent czar.
A hand-winch. Perseverance. Stacks of smoked-fish
Sandwiches in paper. A bunghole. A gill.

The coldest of summers. The alabaster hand
Of snowstorm smothering the humpbacked ridge.
A surfeit of penguins. A tumbling lens.
The slow stretched-out process of harnessing dogs.

Day seven. Finding east. The neverending wind.
Toes, crampons, frostbite; dinner, fishbones, gloom.
Nothingness in sight for five hundred miles.
White expanse unchanging as the weeks go on

And on. The symptoms of madness found in
A canvas tent. The brittle surface of snow
Through which someone plunges and falls. The unmarked
Fork where another takes the wrong path and lands

In neck-deep water. The end of the rope.

This Morning,

The romance of the world washed over me.
My heart swelled with positive feelings, not œdema.
The forklift out the window beeped 'I LUV U' in Morse code.

A curious pigeon molested my birdfeeding contraption.
I pined longingly for my absent biscuits, which had been eaten last week.
Even the unfriendly cat sensed the fragility of the moment
And refrained from licking its bits. How sweet

It was to breathe the sausage-scented air, and feel
The throb of the washing machine like a second heart
Keeping me true. In the garden a host of petunias dangled
And waved their skinny limbs. Oh darlings,

Some days are painted with high-saturation pigment, some
Are faint as a blueprint seen from space – today the bees
Are droning a hosanna to wish me *bonne journée*.

It's ridiculous to be so full of honey for a living.
It's ridiculous how ardently the washing machine sings.
Dear pigeon, I used to be a heretic from the world –
Then romance washed over me. I think I might believe.

Notes

p. 9   'After the Attack of the Crystalline Entity'
The title is a phrase taken from an episode of the TV series *Star Trek: The Next Generation* ('Brothers', written by Rick Berman). The Crystalline Entity was a gigantic creature resembling an ice crystal that could extinguish all the life on a planet at one blow. The poem is in the voice of an android.

p. 10   'Sargent's *The Daughters of Edward D. Boit*'
The Daughters of Edward D. Boit is an 1882 painting by John Singer Sargent. Faneuil Hall (pronounced FAN-you-ull) is an historic building in Boston.

p. 14   'On Being an Android'
'Roomba' is the name of a brand of robotic, self-propelling vacuum cleaners.

p. 15   'Deception Island'
Deception Island, in Antarctica, is regularly visited by modern-day tourists. The British Naval Expedition first conducted a topographic survey of the island in 1829. A base was established there in 1944, but was abandoned following evacuations in 1967 and 1969.

p. 16   'Stag, Exmoor'
The Emperor of Exmoor is a large red stag that was photographed in the Devon countryside and nicknamed by the photographer Richard Austin. It was widely reported to have been killed by a hunter in October 2010, only for observers to claim they spotted it alive a week later.

p. 18   'The Robots'
The phrase 'robo-dwarf hamsters' refers to Roborovski hamsters (also known as robo hamsters or robos), which are the smallest breed of hamster. The Arena Football League is a minor American-football league in the US. Amway is a controversial American direct-sales company. Red Lobster is an American chain of seafood restaurants.

p. 19   'Manet's *Olympia*'
Olympia is an 1863 painting by Edouard Manet.

p. 20   'An American Panda Leaves the National Zoo'
In 2010, a four-year-old panda named Tai Shan was sent to a panda conservation centre in China from the National Zoo in Washington, DC, where it had been born and raised. Previously, the zoo had paid $10 million to the Chinese government for the extended loan of a pair of adult pandas, with the understanding that any cubs produced by them would be permanently relocated to China once they reached breeding age.

p. 25 'The Wyndham Sisters (after Sargent)'
The Wyndham Sisters is an 1899 painting by Sargent.

p. 27 'Walrus'
'Pinniped' is the term for a fin-footed aquatic mammal, a class that includes walruses, seals, and sea lions.

p. 29 'Breaking News'
Mayor McCheese is a character who appeared in American advertisements for the McDonald's restaurant chain; he had a cheeseburger for a head. Cluedo is the board game known as Clue in the US. The reference to Battersea Dogs' Home is meant as a joke; I fully support their work.

p. 31 'Sherlock Holmes on the Trail of the Abominable Snowman'
The word *mishegoss* is Yiddish for 'craziness' or 'nonsense'. 'Lurcher' is the British term for a type of dog, specifically a cross between a sighthound and a collie or terrier. A sledge is known as a sled or sleigh in American English.

p. 38 'Scenes from *My Life as the Abominable Snowman*'
The phrase *no muy guapa* is Spanish for 'not very pretty'.

p. 43 'Five Years Ago,'
Williamsburg and Bethnal Green are neighbourhoods in New York City and London, respectively.

p. 46 'Pet Rescue'
Pet Rescue was a British daytime TV series that showed pets and numerous other animals being rescued from harm, cared for, and rehomed or returned to the wild. Honeysuckle Farm was one of the locations featured on the programme.

p. 50 'The Balbi Children (after Van Dyck)'
The Balbi Children is a painting by Anthony Van Dyck, dated around 1625–7. It was in fact painted in Genoa, not Naples.

p. 51 'Pendant to "The Balbi Children"'
In art history terminology, a pendant is a companion piece, a painting intended to hang together with another. The poem is very loosely inspired by the 1623 painting *Portrait of Marchesa Elena Grimaldi*, by Van Dyck.

p. 56 'The Body in the Library'
The title is taken from a 2007 exhibition by the painter Kirsten Glass at the gallery V22 Ashwin Street in London. It is also the title of a novel by Agatha Christie.

p. 58   'This Morning,'

'Œdema' (spelled 'edema' in American English) is the medical term for an abnormal accumulation of fluid in an organ or tissues, resulting in swelling. The phrase *bonne journée* is French for 'have a nice day'.